Where Does Come From?

Christine Finochio • Jennette MacKenzie

Ben and Dad had been shopping. Ben looked at all the things they had bought. He wondered where all the food came from.

"Dad, where does all this food we bought come from?" asked Ben.

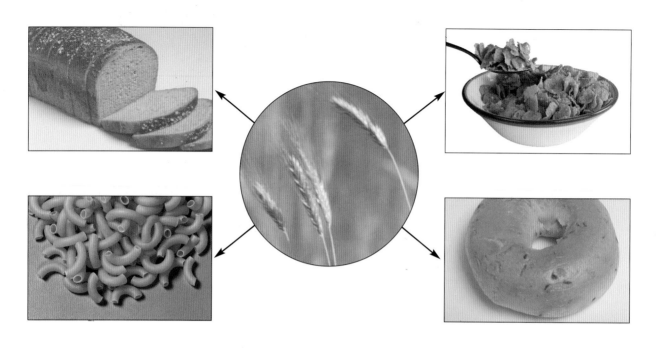

Dad said, "The bread, cereal, pasta, and bagels are all made from the same thing. They're made from grain.

Grain grows in fields. Wheat is one kind of grain. Flour is made from wheat. Flour is used to make bread."

"I think I know where the carrots come from," said Ben. "They grow in the ground."

"Yes," said Dad. "Some vegetables grow underground, like potatoes and carrots. Other vegetables grow above ground, like lettuce and peppers.

flower

flower

We eat the flowers of some vegetables. When we eat cauliflower and broccoli, we're eating the flowers of those plants," said Dad.

stalk

"We eat the stalks of some vegetables,
like celery," said Dad. "We eat many parts
of vegetables.

We also eat fruit. Some fruits grow on trees," said Dad.

"I know," said Ben. "Peaches, apples, oranges, and bananas grow on trees."

"Do you know any fruits that grow on the ground?" asked Dad. Ben couldn't think of any, so Dad helped him.

"Strawberries, blueberries, and watermelons grow on the ground," said Dad.

Dad put some milk in the refrigerator. Ben put ice cream, yogurt, and cheese in the refrigerator. "All those foods come from milk," said Dad.

"Cows make milk," said Ben.

"Milk is used to make many things," said Dad.

Dad put some meat, chicken, and fish into the refrigerator.

"All of these things come from animals," said Dad.

Dad and Ben were
so busy talking,
they didn't notice
that they'd put
away all their
groceries!

"Well," said Dad.
"I guess we won't
have to go
shopping again
for a long time!"